CELEBRATING LIFE TOGETHER

Moira MacManus IBVM

CELEBRATING LIFE TOGETHER

Prayer Services for Primary Schools

VERITAS

First published 1995 by
Veritas Publications
7-8 Lower Abbey Street
Dublin 1

ISBN 1 85390 298 5

**British Library Cataloguing
in Publication Data.
A catalogue record for
this book is available
from the British Library.**

Design: Bill Bolger
Printed in the Republic of Ireland by Betaprint Ltd, Dublin

Contents

Acknowledgements

I want first and foremost to give a really big 'thanks' to the present staff of Loreto Abbey Primary School, Dalkey. At no time did they refuse to co-operate in helping me with this selection. All I had to do was call on them and I have been really touched by their generous co-operation and response. So, thanks for continued support in my years working with you.

Initially, when I got the idea of compiling this collection I was a bit reluctant to take it on board, wondering how viable a product it would be. However, my tutor gave me great encouragement and support, and so, to Mary McPhilipps, a 'tutor' in more ways than one, I extend heartfelt thanks for the push.

My own community watched and listened from the sidelines – some typing numbers, others checking lists, some having to endure the noise of tapes being played over and over again, and all quietly supportive and interested – so a big thanks to them all. To all those who listened to my grumbles, frustrations and queries at times – thanks.

Finally – I left her last deliberately – Estelle McGoldrick IBVM, my typist, who cannot say 'no'. I want to thank her sincerely and warmly for being so willing, despite other numerous demands, to have a go at this. In Ecclesiasticus 6:4 we read: 'a faithful friend is a rare treasure'. Estelle is one of these. Thank you for your faithfulness and loyalty to me all these years.

I hope no one who has been part of this production has been left out. My inspiration was children and hopefully some courageous people will undertake to realise these celebrations with children who know better than all of us how to really celebrate ... and let those of us who are no longer children allow the child in us out to:

Join in Celebrating

Life Together.

Introduction

School is about life and life is what impinges on us as human beings on many different levels – physical, emotional, spiritual and social.

To be human is to feel, experience and acknowledge all the joys, sorrows, losses, pains, excitements and questions with which reality presents us. For this to happen we need to come apart or take time out. A long retreat or a short holiday is not always necessary. What we sometimes need is a good liturgical celebration. We need times where groups of people with common ties, connections and experiences gather together to celebrate the realities of everyday life. You may ask: But why celebrations for school? I say: Why not?

School is one place where you have very many people in large numbers. Where you have people you have moments of life and death. These moments come in all shapes and manifestations. Life is no respecter of persons, status or social background. It caresses and buffets all indiscriminately.

Teachers know from day-to-day experience that within one five-minute stretch the joyful news of the newborn sibling can mingle with that of the heartbreaking loss of a parent or grandparent. Alongside these can be the shattering experience of Mam or Dad leaving or, for many today, the terrible tragedy that Mam or Dad is unlikely to work again. There are happy moments too – birthdays, christenings, parties, holidays, outings. All these can be high or low points in all our lives. We sometimes believe that children are not capable of experiencing the heights or depths of these important events. I believe children are very much aware and that we do not give them credit for the depth of their feelings in all the aspects of life in which they are immersed. In fact, unlike their elders, who are encumbered with the hustle and bustle of living, they are much more likely to be open to all that happens to them negatively or positively.

And so this book. I have taught for many years in the primary school system. Many, many times I have felt the need for the whole school community to come together to celebrate the life of the school. A place to come and share together the triumphs and failures, the joys and sorrows, the hopes and dreams of school life as it is. A place where reality can be connected to what is deepest in us, what ultimately makes any sense of our lives and living, so beautifully described by Patrick Kavanagh in his poem 'The Great Hunger':
> God is in the bits and pieces of
> Everyday ...
> A kiss here and a laugh again
> and sometimes tears ...

And so I put together these selections for *Celebrating Life Together*, to encourage other teachers and group leaders to take the risk of coming together to celebrate their lives with those children they so lovingly tend in all their daily encounters. Go for it. You won't be sorry.

Moira MacManus, IBVM
25 March 1995
Feast of the Annunciation

Suggestions for the Organisation of Celebrations

These are just hints, suggestions, options and ideas for those willing to undertake planning and implementing the services. Each school has its own way of proceeding on occasions like these, so far be it from me to decide for any other group what they should or should not do. The following are merely guidelines as to what could be done to avoid heartache, strain, tension, and valuable time being wasted.

1. Plan in good time. Use the checklists for each service on pages 7-8.

2. Involve as many classes as possible.

3. Select, volunteer, invite or coerce someone who is willing to act as co-ordinator – this role is re-negotiable each time.

4. The co-ordinator selects or invites a small group to work with him or her.

5. Staff must be kept informed and involved throughout the preparation.

6. The group which has been formed chooses the theme for the service at the first meeting and delegates the areas of responsibility, i.e.
   – classes who will be responsible for art work/music/drama/movement
   – classes who will be responsible for readings/poems/prayers
The principal or leaders may be needed depending on which liturgy is being celebrated.

7. The group can plan the liturgy from the selections provided and adapt them according to particular circumstances.

8. Each school decides whether or not to invite local clergy/chaplain/minister/vicar/families/maintenance people. Some services are more appropriate than others for this and it is always wise to avoid inviting people to performances.

9. Meet to tie up loose ends and to co-ordinate the final presentation before the actual service.

10. Follow the celebration with a little 'eats' celebration in a classroom or outdoors!

11. Play quiet music before and after the service.

12. Decide at the beginning of the school year which services are suitable for particular times and organise co-ordinators for them.

13. Remember that these celebrations can be re-arranged, added to or subtracted from, shortened or lengthened. Anything which is suitable or appropriate in each situation can be included, especially appropriate material in the **Children of God** series.

Note: The references for the hymns and songs used throughout are to the **Children of God** teachers' books.

Checklist

1. Celebrating the beginning of the School Year

Checklist
- bible/incense/candles
- matches
- photographs of new children
- photographs of holiday activities
- poems on the theme
- badges for projects
- hymns taught
- leaders/readers/delegation to specific classes

2. Celebrating All Saints/Halloween

Checklist
- bible
- name tags for all children
- poems
- Halloween collage/masks
- hymns taught
- leaders/readers/delegation to specific classes

3. Celebrating the Lives of People in our Families and Friends who have Died

Checklist
- Easter candle/large candle
- matches
- large cloth
- photographs/memorial cards/mementoes of dead relatives and friends
- hymns taught
- leaders/readers/delegation to specific classes

4. Pre–Christmas Celebration

Checklist
- Christmas Tree
- Crib
- decorations
- balloons
- Advent Wreath/Jesse Tree
- bible
- placards
- hampers/toys/gifts
- hymns taught
- leaders/readers/delegation to specific classes

5. Celebrating our Birthdays

Checklist
- lists of class birthdays
- balloons
- collage of birthday cards
- imitation presents
- photographs of birthday parties
- real/imitation birthday cake
- music

–   matches
–   hymns taught
–   leaders/readers/delegation to specific classes

6.   Celebrating the Life of Mary

Checklist
–   icon
–   statue
–   candles/incense/flowers
–   matches
–   posters/collage of children's images of Mary
–   hymns taught
–   video of Mary or children dramatising an event in Mary's life
    leaders/readers/delegation to specific classes

7.   Easter Celebration

Checklist
–   large Easter collage
–   Cross
–   purple cloth
–   hymns taught
–   Easter candle lit/matches
–   flowers/incense/stones
–   percussion instruments
–   poems
–   Easter egg
–   Easter bunny
–   photographs of new life
–   leaders/readers/delegation to specific classes

8.   Celebrating our Call to help People in Need

Checklist
–   collage of places of need
–   large banner – 'Whatsoever you do'
–   Trócaire posters/boxes
–   hymns taught
–   stories
–   a person from a needy area
–   a video of a needy place/places
–   baskets for collection
–   leaders/readers/delegation to specific classes

9.   Celebrating the End of Another School Year

Checklist
–   class work for exhibition
–   video of the year's events
–   decorated school hall
–   photographs
–   candle
–   matches
–   hymns taught
–   leaders/readers/delegation to specific classes

1. Celebrating the beginning of the school year

Preparation
Meet to co-ordinate the service. Choose the theme for the service:
> *1. Let's be friends together.*
> *2. Our school is a happy place to be.*
> *3. We will be welcoming to all who come to our school.*
> *4. We will think of the lonely in our school this year.*
> *5. We will look after those who are frightened this year.*

SECTION I

All the children congregate in the school hall, class by class.
The hall is already decorated with photos of summer activities/seaside/games/
swimming/tennis/ picnics/boats/planes/cars/bicycles. Adapt to the area you are serving.

Place a bible and incense with candles as the centrepiece in the hall.
Display photographs of all the new children on the walls.
The theme for the year could be illustrated on a big banner.

Hymn
'All the Ends of the Earth', **Workers for the Kingdom,** *page 87*
After the hymn all sit on the floor.

Introduction
Welcome the children back. Call on all the new children to stand up and be welcomed to the school, then sit again. Continue as you wish: the dreams for this school year, sadness because the holidays are over, the standards for which the school is renowned – kindness, caring, consideration for others, politeness, looking after the new and lost – and hopes for the school year ahead. Link to the theme chosen for this new school year.

All stand.
'Sing to the Mountains', **Workers for the Kingdom,** *page 77 (using percussion)*

All sit.

Reading
About beginnings John 1:1-5
(or any appropriate poem or reflection on the theme of beginnings)

Response
Lord, help us as we begin again.

1. For those beginning school for the first time. ℟
2. For those beginning another school year. ℟
3. For those beginning to teach another school year. ℟
4. For those beginning in a new school. ℟
5. For those beginning to prepare to leave our school at the end of the year. ℟
6. For those who have just left our school and are beginning in a new school at this time.℟
7. For all those who take care of us and are beginning another year of taking us to and collecting us from school, helping and protecting us. ℟

11

All stand.
Together let us join hands and sing to God our Father who cares for each one of us.
Have the group mime it or do it to movement.

All say the 'Our Father' together.

SECTION 2

All sit.
Have a group from 4th, 5th or 6th class read short stories of how they spent the summer holidays, or read poems about it.

Pause.
All close your eyes.

One child
1. Remember the picnics we had over the summer. *Pause*
2. Remember the happy days at the beach. *Pause*
3. Remember the trips to the amusements, town, down/up the country, to visit friends or relations. *Pause*
4. Remember going in the car, the aeroplane, the boat, the bicycle, the van. *Pause*
5. Remember the fights. *Pause*

Leader
Join hands and say together:
Thank you God our Father for all the people we were with during the summer.
We remember especially those who helped make our summer a happy and joyful time.
Look after them all; we pray that they will enjoy a good year ahead too.

SECTION 3

Commissioning Service of Prefects

All sit.

CONCLUDING SECTION

Wishing the staff and pupils well. Call out the names of class prefects, and present each one with some form of badge, commissioning them to care for the children under their care in the coming year.

All stand.

Final Prayer

**Principal/
Vice-principal**
Father, Mother, God ... we entrust all these children created in your image and likeness to your loving care this coming year. Bless each one of them and all their families. Enlighten our teachers to tend each child on their journey of life. May everyone who comes to visit our school experience a warm, welcoming, happy atmosphere here. We ask this in the name of Jesus Your Son.

Final Hymn
'*I Will be with You*', **Walk in My Presence**, *page 145*

2. Celebrating All Saints/Halloween

Preparation
Meet to co-ordinate the service. Decorate the hall with names of a variety of saints. Have two or more classes involved in the preparation of the Halloween collage, masks and name tags.

SECTION 1

Gathering
The children assemble wearing name tags.

Leader   **Welcome and Introduction**

Ask the children to look at their own name and the names of the children on each side of them. Then, having organised the following in advance, have several children (about three) from each class in order and call out their names. The leader then refers to the origin of Christian names, that when we were baptised we usually received the name of someone who loved and served God very much. We believe that these people, called saints, are now continuing to help us in heaven.

Junior Classes   *All stand and sing 'I have a Name', **Show us the Father**, page 156*

All sit.
Children from one or two classes present a short sketch or life of two well-known saints of choice, e.g. Patrick/Brigid/Thérèse/Bernadette/Francis of Assisi.

In response to this, either the whole school (or just the class in whose programme the hymn occurs) stands and sings a hymn related to the sketch chosen.

Hymns
*'A Bhríd A Mhuire na nGael', **Workers for the Kingdom**, page 98; 'Saint Francis', **Walk in Love**, page 219; 'Queen Margaret', **Walk in Love**, page 221; 'Lúireach Phádraig', **Walk in Love**, page 226; 'Dóchas Linn Naomh Pádraig', **Workers for the Kingdom**, page 131; 'Brother Sun and Sister Moon', **Workers for the Kingdom**, p.76.*

All sit.

SECTION 2

Reading
I have called you by name   Isaiah 43:1-3 *(Children's bible version, if possible)*

Leader   *Talk about the origin of Halloween, the old Celtic festival celebrating the spirits of dead descendants, and how this became christianised as our modern feasts of All Saints and All Souls. (Check out and fill out this knowledge, linking to masks/bonfires, etc. Read note on page 33.)*

The children may respond with poem(s) on Halloween (own choice) in Irish or English.

All stand.

Prayers

℟   We praise you, God, for all our saints.

Child 1	We pray for all the new babies born this past year who have been named after these people who loved and served you all their lives and we pray that they too will spend their lives doing good and serving others in your name. ℟
Child 2	We pray for all those who died this year and who joined those saints whose names they were given. ℟
Child 3	We pray for all our favourite aunts and uncles whom we are called after. We hope that we will take on the good qualities they inspire in us. ℟
Child 4	We pray for our parents and hope that we will continue to carry their good name as we live lives of truth, honesty and compassionate love. ℟
Child 5	We pray for ourselves, our friends and our teachers. We ask you, Jesus, who called each one by name – Mary, Peter, Simon – to help us to become 'real' saints to our families, our classmates and pupils. ℟
Child 6	We all have heroes in our lives, people whose qualities of courage, bravery, determination, persistence and goodness inspire us. Help us, Lord, to become like them. We pray that there may always be heroes, earthly ones who will lead us to become other people's heroes in turn. ℟
Leader	We gather all our prayers in the name of all the saints and of our own favourite ones, and pray to God our Father in the way Jesus named him.

All stand.

All sing the 'Our Father' (actions optional).

Leader/
Principal

Final Prayer
Lord God, as we celebrate Halloween and All Saints, we remember all the dead generations past from Celtic times and beyond. We look forward to having a great Halloween filled with joy, excitement and fun. We thank you for the inspiring lives of all these people who dedicated their lives to you. We pray that we too will make full use of the gifts you have given each one of us to become the people you created us to become.

All stand.

Hymn
*All sing 'If God is for us', **Workers for the Kingdom**, page 258*

3. Celebrating the Lives of People in our Families and Friends who have Died

Preparation
Meet to co-ordinate the service. Decorate the hall with photos, stories and memorial cards of the children's dead relatives and friends. Place an Easter candle or any large candle as the centre-piece. This should be lit before the service begins. A cloth should be laid on the ground for the children's mementoes.

SECTION 1

Leader
(Teacher/
Principal)

Introduction

All sit.

We are gathered here today in this month of November to remember in love all our dead relatives and friends. November is called the month of the Holy Souls, and we believe that just as Jesus died and rose again to share his new life with God the Father, so too are all our friends and relatives happily living their new life with God.

All stand.

Hymn
'Though the Mountains May Fall', **Walk in My Presence**, *page 187*

All sit.

Reading
Romans 6:5-11 *(or any other suitable reading)*

Litany of Response

℞   We pray that they are all very happy.

1.   For all our grannies and grandads who have died. ℞
2.   For any of our friends or relations who died during the past year. ℞
3.   For anyone who died alone. ℞
4.   For anyone who died suddenly. ℞
5.   For anyone who died as a result of an accident at home or on the road or at sea. ℞

Prayer
Lord, we ask you to take all our friends and relations into your loving care. You know how much we miss them and love them. Take care of them as they took care of us and grant them your happiness always.

All stand.

Hymn
'Jesus, Remember Me', **Workers for the Kingdom**, *page 143*

All sit.

Ritual of Goodbye

Any child who has had a relative or friend die could have with them a picture or story or something belonging to the person, or something symbolic.

Leader
(Teacher/pupil)

When people we love come to visit we say goodbye to them when they are leaving. Sometimes we cry because we do not like to see them going. We want them to stay. We want to be able to talk to them or see them or be with them, and so saying goodbye is very hard. But if we do not say goodbye we are not allowing those people to live their lives fully. We are holding on to them and sometimes this can make them sad. The same applies when those we love die. We want them to be really happy but we want them still to be alive. We cry, we get angry, we keep hoping we will hear them, or that it is not true, or that it is all a big mistake and we will see them again. But that does not happen when people die. They do not come back again. We get very lonely. We miss them because we loved them so much and we need to say goodbye so that we will know they will be happy and not sad for us. We know they are with us always. They never go far away. They will always be there to help us like guardian angels. So now, all those who would like to say goodbye, come up with photos, paintings, or any other keepsake you might have made, and we will place it on the centrepiece and silently say goodbye.

While this is happening sing 'I Will be With You', **Walk in My Presence,** *page 145, until each child has finished.*

All stand.

Leader/
Principal   **Final Prayer**

Lord, lead into your Kingdom all our friends and relatives. May they have their own special place in your heavenly home where they will all be as happy as can be
(in silence, we all remember our own dead).

All   Eternal rest give unto them, O Lord, and let perpetual light shine upon them. May they rest in peace. Amen.

Final Hymn
'Be Still My Soul', **Workers for the Kingdom,** *page 424*

4. Pre-Christmas Celebration

Preparation
Meet to co-ordinate the service. Decorate the school hall or assembly point with a Christmas tree, crib, decorations, cards, balloons, class work etc.

Assemble at a spot outside this area with an Advent Wreath and/or a Jesse Tree.

Section 1

The children stand waiting.

Leader	What are we waiting for? *Pause*
Child 1	Why are we waiting? *Pause*
Child 2	Why are we still waiting? *Pause*
Child 3	What is keeping us out here? *Pause*
Child 4	I hate waiting. *Pause*
Child 5	I get butterflies in my tummy when I'm waiting in the dentist's. *Pause*
Child 6	I get sick with excitement when I'm waiting for my birthday party to begin. *Pause*
Child 7	I get anxious when one of my family does not come home from school at the usual time. *Pause*

Vary the above to suit circumstances.
or
The children could have placards scattered around the ground bearing the words: We're waiting. *They could chorus the words every so often.*
Selected children ask: 'And what are you waiting for?' The same reply is repeated: 'We're waiting for the Promised Saviour'.
Crash of tambourines, drums, any percussion instruments. The speaker begins in loud voice: (read slowly)
A child will be born in Israel, and his name will be called Emmanuel.

Hymn
'O Come, O Come, Emmanuel', **Walk in My Presence**, *page 171*

Section 2

Shepherds arrive announcing their news: A baby, a Saviour has been born in a stable.

Reading
The people who walked in darkness Isaiah 9
The children begin to move towards the hall or assembly point and/or can sing:

'The Light of Christ', **Grow in Love**, *page 180*

All arrive and settle. All sit.

Activity
1. *Have a class present a short Christmas Play or*
2. *Have a Carol Concert or*
3. *Have a Christmas Concert with participation from each class in the school, involving mime, poetry, song, dance or*
4. *Stage a liturgical movement based on a Christmas carol or*
5. *Read a reflection based on the Christmas story or*
6. *Have about four children telling about 'Christmas in our house', or children from abroad telling about 'Christmas in my country' or*
7. *Continue with the Prayer Service.*

All sit.

Leader The theme is 'Christmas is a time for giving'. God gave his Son to us to help us to know him and love him, and his Son Jesus asked us over and over again to love one another. We show our love when we give ourselves even when we are tired or weary. This Christmas we will try to:

Child 1 Give a smile to an old person we might not like.

Child 2 Do a message for our mammy/granny when we might prefer to go out to play with our friends or watch TV or a video.

Child 3 Give a hug to a baby cousin/sister/brother who looks sad or lonely or who is upset or crying.

Child 4 Give a present to those I love.

Child 5 Give help around the house at Christmas time.

Child 6 Remember to say Happy Birthday to Jesus on his Birthday.

Child 7 Remember to say thanks.

Child 8 And now we give our gifts for those who may not get as much as we do.

A group of the children carry up toys, food and parcels.

As the children carry up gifts each one describes what is being carried up and where the gifts are going to.

Leader **Concluding prayer**
All stand.

As we wait in hope for the coming birthday of Jesus, we pray for our families, we pray for our friends, we pray for our relatives who are coming home for Christmas.
We pray for all the children who will be spending Christmas in hospital and for all those who are sad or lonely this Christmas.
We pray that people everywhere will experience some of the joy, peace and happiness that Jesus promised when he came, and we wish everyone a Happy Christmas.

Finale
All sing, 'We wish you a merry Christmas'
or a selection of Christmas songs & carols

18

5. Celebrating our Birthdays

Preparation

Meet to co-ordinate the service. Each class could make out lists of birthdays and one of the senior classes could collate them so that the walls of the school hall are decorated with lists of birthdays of all the children from January to December.
Write down the full names. No dates are needed, e.g.:

January	February	March	April	May	June
Mary Brown					

The hall could be decorated with balloons, a collage of birthday cards, imitation presents, photos of birthday parties. The centrepiece should be a real or imitation birthday cake with lighted candles. (The co-ordinator/team could delegate various classes to produce all these items.)

All the school congregates in the hall.
Music could be playing softly (tape).
All stand quietly in the birthday atmosphere.
As the music ends the children sit.

The leader introduces the theme of birthdays.

Leader   All of us have birthdays. For some it is only a few years ago, for others a bit longer, and for some of us it is a long, long time ago that we would rather forget! But we must remember that on the day we were born we were given as a great gift to our families. We were born because we are precious, a gift of love and life. We were given life to talk, shout and sing and we come to celebrate all our birthdays today.

All sit.

Reading
A child from a senior class should read this:

I have called you by name   Isaiah 43:1. 4. 13

I have called you by Name
You are mine.
You are precious to me
Do not be afraid because
I love you.
I am God and always will be.
Before I formed you in the
womb I knew you
And I will never forget you.

All stand.

All sing   *'Glory and Praise to Our God'*, **Walk in My Presence**, *page 350*

All sit.

Leader   All the children whose birthdays are in January, February or March, stand, and the rest of the school will sing Happy Birthday to them. *Pause*

Prayer
For all the children whose birthdays fall in January, February or March, we pray that they will have a great birthday full of surprises and lovely presents.

All sing   'O, Lord, Hear my Prayer', **Walk in Love**, *page 133*

Leader   These children sit. Children with birthdays in April, May or June stand, and everyone will sing 'Happy Birthday' to them. *Pause*

Prayer
For all these children whose birthday is in April, May or June, we pray that they will receive lots of cards, love and surprises.

All sing   'O, Lord, Hear my Prayer'. *Pause*

Leader   These children sit. Children who celebrate their birthday in July, August or September stand, and the group will sing 'Happy Birthday'. *Pause*

Prayer
For all the children who celebrate their birthdays during the summer holidays and the first month back at school, we want to remember them and hope they have a really good, enjoyable birthday.

All sing   'O, Lord, Hear my Prayer'.

Leader   The last group, those with birthdays in October, November or December, stand, and everyone will sing 'Happy Birthday'. *Pause*

Prayer
We pray for these children who celebrate their birthdays during October, November and December, and wish them a really happy day filled with happy memories and surprises.

All sing   'O, Lord, Hear my Prayer'.

Leader   Conclusion
Light the candle if it has not been lit.
Today we will all celebrate each other's birthday and join hands and sing:

All sing   'Sing to the Mountains', **Workers for the Kingdom**, *page 77*

6. Celebrating the Life of Mary

This can be used in October – the month of the Rosary, or May – the month of Our Lady, or on any Feast of Mary.

Preparation
Meet to co-ordinate the service. Arrange a display of the following in the hall: statue; icon; posters/collage; candles; incense; flowers. There could be a short video of the story of Knock/Lourdes/Fatima to hand.

SECTION 1

Ask all to sit except the Infant classes, who will sing together:

'Jesus was a Baby', **You are my Friends,** *page 102 (Play tape to accompany them if necessary.)*

Clap the children at end to affirm them; then they too sit.

Leader	We are here today to celebrate the life of Mary the Mother of Jesus. The Infant classes have sung to us so beautifully and have told us that Mary cared for Jesus since the day he was born, just like our Mammies have cared for us.
	How do Mammies care for us?
Child 1	They keep us clean.
Child 2	They make sure we have enough to eat.
Child 3	They check our homework.
Child 4	They hug us and love us when we are sad or lonely.
Child 5	They check us when we are naughty or misbehaving.
Leader	Do you think Mary did these things for Jesus? Of course she did. She washed him, fed him, checked his homework. Remember, when he wandered off during a trip she said that she and Joseph were very concerned and asked him why he had run off. She cared very much for him all her life.
	We will now see occasions where Mary looked after and cared for Jesus.

A video of a short dramatisation performed by the children could now be shown, using the following incidents in life of Mary (See pages 34-41):

- *The Annunciation of the birth of Jesus*
- *Mary tells Joseph her predicament*
- *The journey to Bethlehem with Joseph*
- *The birth of Jesus*
- *The child Jesus is found in the Temple*
- *A day in the life of Mary and Jesus at 4 yrs/7 yrs/10 yrs*
- *Mary meets Jesus on the road to Calvary*
- *Mary stands by the Cross of Jesus*

- *Mary watches the men taking Jesus' body down*
- *Mary is told the news of Jesus' Resurrection*
- *A glimpse at Mary's life after Jesus died*

Choose about four or five of the above and represent them either on video or on stage.

All stand.

All sing   'Mary, Mother of Jesus', **Show us the Father**, *page 104*

SECTION 2   *(Sections 2 or 3 or both can be used here.)*

Have a selection of children from the upper classes acting as Mary, and dressed accordingly, scattered around the hall.

Child 1   I am Mary, and when I was at home with my Mammy I used to ... *let them continue by themselves with a few sentences.*

Child 2   I am Mary, and when I went out to play with my friends we would ... *continue*

Child 3   I am Mary, and when I went to school I would ... *continue*

Child 4   I am Mary, and the night I was told that I would be the mother of Jesus, I ..... *continue*

Child 5   I am Mary, and when I saw the people at the Wedding Feast without wine, I .... *continue*

Child 6   I am Mary, and when I saw the soldiers beating Jesus, I ... *continue*

In response, all stand and say together one of the Joyful Mysteries (in Irish or in English)

All sing   'Mary, Will you take this Baby Boy?', **Show us the Father**, *page 105*
or
'Holy Mary, Full of Grace', **Workers for the Kingdom**, *page 415*
or
'The Bakerwoman', **Walk in My Presence**, *page 470*

SECTION 3

All sit.

Show a video of the story of Knock or Lourdes or Fatima.

All stand.

Litany of Mary

Leader   The response is: Pray for us.

Mary who cared for Jesus. ℞
Mary who has appeared in many places. ℞
Mary who helped the people at the wedding. ℞
Mary who was afraid when Jesus got lost. ℞
Mary who checked Jesus. ℞

Mary who celebrated birthdays with Jesus. ℞

Mary who hugged Jesus when he was sad or lonely or hurt. ℞

Mary who watched Jesus die. ℞

Mary who is now with Jesus protecting us all. ℞

Mary, a beautiful woman and mother. ℞

All sing   *'Hail Mary', **Walk in Love,** page 277*

Leader   **Concluding Prayer**

Mary, Máire, Muireann, Muire and other names that mean Mary, we ask you to continue to care for us, protect us and guide us to become the fully alive Christian people that we were created to become. Help each one of us to listen to the voice of God within us calling us to be the unique people we are meant to be. May your courage, faith and strength continue to inspire us to respond as you did. We ask you this in the name of your Son, Jesus, to whom you gave life, support, strength and protection.

All stand.

Concluding Hymn

All sing   *'Holy Mary, Full of Grace'* **Workers for the Kingdom,** *page 415 (or any other suitable hymn)*

7. Easter Celebration – Jesus is Risen, Alleluia!

Preparation

Meet to co-ordinate the service. The theme of the service is 'Alleluia, Jesus is Risen'. Outline the plan and delegate participants to leading/reading roles. A large collage of the Resurrection scene could be facing the children as they enter the hall.

SECTION 1

The whole school gathers at a Cross set up elsewhere, covered in purple and surrounded creatively with candles, stones etc.

The children stand around the Cross. Choose one of following suggestions for this section:

- *Dramatise the Seven Last Words*
- *Read and enact the journey from the Garden*
- *Enact the conversation between:*
  the soldier and Jesus
  the thief and Jesus
  the women and Jesus
  Mary and Jesus ...
- *Begin the final journey and dramatise a few stations in a modern version.*
- *Move from the adulation of Palm Sunday to the denunciation of Good Friday. Intersperse with 'Stay With Me',* **Walk in Love***, page 254 or, 'Jesus Remember Me',* **Workers for the Kingdom***, page 143*

Instructions to the children

All curl up and become dead; silence; pause.

Begin to return slowly – hands, feet, body, eyes open – stand and begin to move towards the hall.

As they enter the hall the Easter Candle should be lit. Flowers, incense and a backdrop, hanging or collage should already be in place.

SECTION 2

The children stand quietly until all are assembled.
Then:
1. *re-enact the story of the women (pages 50-51);*
2. *re-enact the story of Mary of Magdala (page 51) or*
3. *have either story read by separate voices*

Follow this by having everyone stand, singing joyously, using percussion instruments, etc,. There should be plenty of jubilation.

All sing   *'Christ is Alive',* **Workers for the Kingdom***, page 321*

All sit.

One of the children could read an Easter poem.

Have a table in the hall with the following arranged on it:
a Cross, an Easter Egg, an Easter Bunny, and other symbols of choice on the theme 'New Life',
i.e. photographs of new babies, lambs, chickens, rabbits.

The children remain seated.

SECTION I
Allocate one child to each symbol. They should move forward and pick up their symbol, e.g. the
Cross, and hold it up, saying something like the following.

Child 1   This Cross reminds us of what Jesus did for us. He died for us because he wants us all to live the new life with him and his Father. We pray for those people we know who died this year, and we pray that they are enjoying eternal life with Jesus and his Father.
Lord, hear us.

Child 2   *(picks up an Easter Egg)*
This Easter Egg is full of sweets and is made of chocolate. We all look forward to enjoying eggs like this on Easter Sunday. Help us, Lord, to share our eggs with those who will receive none and to give a piece to people who visit, just like Jesus gave his life for his friends.
Lord, hear us.

Child 3   *(picks up an Easter Bunny)*
This Easter Bunny reminds us of all the newly-born little bunny rabbits tearing around happily these days. We pray that we will always respect new life in the animal world and treat each little fragile animal with care, love and reverence.
Lord, hear us.

Child 4   *(picks up a photo of a new baby)*
This photograph reminds us of the new babies born this year. Each one of us was a little baby like this once, born to bring life, love and happiness to our families. We pray that all new babies will receive the love, care and attention they need to grow and become full human beings.
Lord, hear us.

CONCLUDING SECTION

Leader   All stand.

With joy in the Risen Christ we will all pray together that this Easter we will share in the joys of the Risen Christ, as we sing:

'Our Father' .... (with movement if possible)

**Leader/
Principal**   **Concluding Prayer**

Lord, Jesus, we have spent Lent doing things to try to become better people. Sometimes we failed and we started again because you encouraged us when you said 'the just one falls seven times'. We thank you for helping us to start again each time we were tempted to give up ... and we look forward now to sharing the joys of your Resurrection as we celebrate Easter this year.

All   **HAPPY EASTER!**

Final Hymn
*'He is Lord', **Grow in Love**, page 239*

8. Celebrating our Call to Help People in Need

Preparation
Meet to co-ordinate the service. The hall could be sectioned, as follows:

1. *Area for the needy abroad, e.g. Africa, and in Ireland, e.g. the homeless and the unemployed.*

2. *Area for the needy at home, e.g. those who are, sad, lonely, vulnerable, depressed. (Be sensitive to the children's circumstances.)*

Display a collage of any or all of the above, and a banner bearing the words 'Whatsoever you do to the least of my people'. Plan the service to coincide with People in Need Day, Telethon or the Trócaire Lenten Collection, and have the children prepared in advance for a collection to be taken up during the service for a specific need. Have some children dressed in the garb of the needy in the freeze position.

SECTION 1

The children gather in the previously arranged hall.

All stand.

Leader/ Principal	**Introduction**

Introduce the theme of the celebration referring to banner or posters. We are all gathered together here today to think of those who are in need of our love, care, support and understanding – those people in need who can be as near as members of our own family or as far away as Somalia or Sudan – and so we begin by singing together:

'God's Spirit is in My Heart', **Workers for the Kingdom**, *page 159*

All sit.

Reading
The final judgement, Matthew 25:31-46

This can be read using different voices and sound effects.

All sing   *'O Lord hear My Prayer',* **Walk in Love**, *page 133*

Child 1   For the times we saw you alone or hungry and were too greedy to share.
      ℟ Forgive us, Lord.

Child 2   For the times you needed a coat to keep you warm or shelter you from the rain and we were too selfish to share.
      ℟ Forgive us, Lord.

Child 3   For the times we saw you being held prisoner by bullies and were too afraid to speak up for you.
      ℟ Forgive us, Lord.

26

Child 4	For the times we saw that you were lonely and shy and were too busy looking after ourselves.
	℞ Forgive us, Lord.

Child 5	For the times we held on to our money instead of giving some of it to a good cause.
	℞ Forgive us, Lord.

Child 6	For the times we saw you needing a smile or a hug and we chose to ignore it because of our friends.
	℞ Forgive us, Lord.

Leader	For all those times that we acted out of fear, selfishness or self-centredness and closed our hearts, minds and ears to the cry of the needy, we will ask God now in the next hymn to give us courage to become a true follower of Jesus, who came to bring life, not death, to all.

All stand.

All sing	'Whatsoever You Do', **Walk in My Presence**, page 273

SECTION 2

All sit.

The leader has several options.

– *Have a child/children read/tell stories of children from needy places.*

– *Bring in someone who has worked in an area like Bosnia, South America, Sudan or Somalia to speak about their experiences.*

– *Show video shots of places where there is obvious need.*

– *Have the children enact a day in the life of a child from any of these places.*

– *Have a number of children dress in the garb of each country and have each one tell a little story about himself or herself.*

All stand.

All sing	'Children of the Universe', **Workers for the Kingdom**, page 102

All sit.

Leader/Child	**Reflection**

Who will feed my children
who are hungry everywhere?
Who will clothe my people who are naked?

Who will free my people from the imprisonment of unemployment, violent homes or no education?

Who will give my children the love, affection and care that they need?
Who will be courageous enough to stand up for my oppressed little ones? The orphans of Romania? The parentless of Bosnia? The slaves of the Indians and Chinese?

Who will pray for the people of violence to bring about peace in this war-torn world?

Leader   All stand.

We will respond to these pleas by singing:

All sing   *'Here I am, Lord', **Workers for the Kingdom**, page 407*

As this is being sung collection baskets are passed around and delegated children carry these in procession to a banner of a particular need and place them around it.

CONCLUDING SECTION

All stand.

Leader   We thank you, Lord, for the generosity of all here today who have chosen to give some of their pocket money or savings to help those in need. We hope that our prayers and contributions will do some little good towards alleviating the awfulness of the lives of these needy people. We beg you to give us generous hearts that will always continue to be open to the cry of the needy, so that on the last day we will hear your voice saying: 'Come you, blessed of my Father, into the Kingdom prepared for you, because, as long as we did it to one of the least of your people we did it to you'. We pray for this in the name of all who are needy today. Amen.

Final Hymn
*'Think a Little While', **Workers for the Kingdom**, page 242*

9. Celebrating the End of another School Year

Preparation
Meet to co-ordinate the service. Choose the theme of the service, e.g. 'Thanksgiving'. Each class should exhibit work from their room in the hall. Decorate the hall with pictures of summer and photographs of big school events. Have a video of the year's events: First Confession, Communion, Confirmation, playground/classroom activities, outings, fundraising etc. Place a decorated candle as a centrepiece and light it before the children enter the hall.

SECTION 1

Principal	**Introduction and Welcome**

- *Allow time for the children to wander quietly around the hall, looking at the photographs.*
- *Each child sits quietly when finished.*
- *Now watch the video slowly and give them time to see themselves.*

Leader   The response is: We thank you, Lord, for everything.

All   We thank you, Lord, for everything.

Child 1   Our bodies can do many things: cartwheels, jumps, swimming, walking and running. For all these gifts we thank you, Lord. ℟

Child 2   Each day we come to school with our bags full of books. We have the gifts of our minds to work with these books. For this we thank you, Lord. ℟

Child 3   We go to school each day with lunches in our bags, freshly washed clothes, money for buses and copies. We thank our parents who are so good to us always. For this we thank you, Lord. ℟

Child 4   In school we use our books, pencils and markers under the guidance of our teachers, who have to be very patient with us at times. We thank you for all the encouragement and help given to us by our teachers. For this we thank you, Lord. ℟

Child 5:   Our school is always shining and clean. We thank you God for our cleaners who keep our school and classrooms bright and shining for us. For this we thank you, Lord. ℟

Child 6:   Each day we get safely to school because of our lollipop lady/man. We hope she/he has a good rest and comes back to guide us safely across the road again in September. For this we thank you, Lord. ℟

Child 7   For all our friends *(pause)* who have helped to make school such a happy place for us. We wish them all a good holiday and we look forward to seeing them again in September. For this we thank you, Lord. ℟

Child 8   Finally, we pray for our friends and all those who will be leaving our school and going to other schools. We will miss them and we wish them all the best in their new schools. For this we thank you, Lord. ℟

We thank you, Lord, for all the events of the past year, all that we have looked back on again today: our plays, sports, Communion, Confirmation, outings, fundraising. We thank you for the energy you gave us to put into these. We ask you to bless all those who helped us in any way during these school events. We ask this through Christ Our Lord. Amen.

All stand.

All sing   *'All the ends of the Earth', **Workers for the Kingdom**, page 87*

Love is something if you give it away.

SECTION 2

All sit.
Have a child or a few children speak about their pieces of art work, projects or poems.

Have a selection of poems and stories read.

All stand.

All sing   *'Sing Praise', **Walk in Love**, page 171*

If I had a hammer.

SECTION 3

All sit.

Thanksgiving for the children's gifts

Organise a mini-concert involving:
1. Irish dancing
2. Piano playing
3. Violin solo
4. Class choral
5. Mime
6. All classes involved in a short selection of songs, hymns etc.

Whole world Lord of the dance

CONCLUDING SECTION

Leader/ Principal   We thank you, Lord, for all the gifts we have experienced here today and during the past school year. Bless and protect all these children and their families during the summer break. We pray that each one will come back full of happy memories of their summer and ready to begin another new school year full of energy and enthusiasm. We ask this in the Name of the Father, Son and Holy Spirit.

All stand.

Final Hymn   *Seek and you shall find*
*'Sing to the Mountains', **Workers for the Kingdom**, page 77*

Drama Sketches and Dialogues
to accompany the Celebrations

All Saints/Halloween *(See note on page 35)*

Sketch from the life of St Patrick

THE KIDNAPPING

How it all began ....

Scene 1:	*A group of boys and girls playing a game of football outside – late evening.*
	A cheer goes up.
Spectators:	Hurrah, hurrah, another goal for us. Well done Francis – you'll get on the French team yet.
	The game continues for a short while.
Mother's voice:	Patrick, Patrick and Maria, time for supper.
Patrick:	Ah, just a few minutes more and the game will be over.
Maria:	We could lose if Patrick and I leave now.
Mother:	It's well past your usual time and it's only because you have a free day tomorrow that I've let you stay out this late. Come in at once.
	Patrick and Maria, grumbling, leave the game and come in.
Mother:	Have your wash and get ready for bed, then come for supper.
Patrick & Maria:	Yes, Mama.
Scene 2:	*Around the table*
Mother:	Well, tell us all about your day.
Maria:	We had a great day. First we walked to the forest ...
Patrick:	*(interrupting)* ... Yes, we saw the most beautiful deer there, remember, Maria?
Mother:	Patrick, don't interrupt your sister without saying 'excuse me'.
Patrick:	Sorry, Mama.
Maria:	*(smug)* After that we sat on the rocks and myself and my friends made daisy chains and some went playing hide and seek.
Patrick:	Then we all had a picnic of wild raspberries, and drank from the stream *(yawns)*.
Mother:	I think you've both had quite a day and now it's time for bed. Off you go. I'll be up to read you a story and say your prayers.
Scene 3:	*Patrick's bedroom*
Patrick:	Mama, will you read the story about the pirate who stole the little boy?
Mama:	After we've said our goodnight prayers.
Patrick:	God bless Mama, Papa, Maria, all my friends, grandmama and grandpapa. Thank you, God, for the lovely, happy day. Keep me safe tonight and sorry for being sulky about coming in from my play tonight. Mama, what's God like?

Mother:	God is like a loving father or mother who will always protect you no matter how afraid or lonely or sad or upset you are.
Patrick:	If I got hurt would God know where I am?
Mother:	Of course, my child, God takes care of everything.
Patrick:	Read me the story now, Mama, please.
Mother:	Once upon a time there was a cruel sea-captain whose name was 'Jake the snake'. He spent his life travelling the world and stealing little boys from their houses.
Patrick:	Zzzz *(asleep)*.
Scene 4:	*The Kidnapping. Patrick's bedroom*
	Patrick is asleep in bed, thinking that what's happening to him is a dream.
Robber 1:	Shh!...You clumsy fool. Do you want the whole household on our backs?
Robber 2:	Quick, grab him before he wakes up or screams *(grabs Patrick)*. Now bind his hands and feet.
Robber 3:	We'll get a fine penny for him. Look at the healthy look of him – he'll fetch plenty.
Robber 1:	Carefully now, we'll have to be very quiet. Anything else we can steal here?
Robber 2:	This looks valuable *(picks up a gold inkstand and puts it into his sack. Prowls around.)*
Robber 3:	Come on, I hear noises. Let's get out of here.
	The leave the house with Patrick struggling and fighting to be released.
Scene 5:	*Market for selling children*
Patrick:	*(quietly to himself)* It's not a dream, it's for real. I'm being sold. Poor Papa and Mama must be terribly worried about me. I'll be really brave and the first chance I get I'll escape. I must remember what Mama said, God's always there looking after me. I'll talk to God as my friend.
Seller:	Boy for sale! Fine strong, strapping boy for sale! Any buyers? 150 francs?
Man in crowd:	He looks terrified. He is about the same age as my boy, not much more. I'll buy him and be gentle to him. 100 francs!
Seller:	Going, going, gone to the gentleman for 100 francs.
Narrator:	Patrick was put on board a boat with other young people, not knowing where he was going. The ship landed at Carlingford Lough and he was put on the mountain of Sliabh Mish to care for swine. His home was a cave in the side of the mountain. He continued to remember the words of his mother that God would always look after him, so he prayed every time he was lonely or sad or afraid. He came to realise that the people who lived in this strange country did not know about this loving God in whom he believed and he promised himself that if he ever became free he would come back as a priest to this country and talk to the people about his God. And that is what he did and that is why he is now the Patron Saint of Ireland. He brought the good news to the people of Ireland that we have a God who loves, cares for and protects us every day of our lives, from the moment we are born to the hour of our death.

34

A Note on the Origin of Halloween

THE CELTIC LINK BETWEEN HALLOWEEN AND THE FEAST OF 1 NOVEMBER

Samhain is the Celtic feast of 1 November. Considerable obscurity surrounds the selection of 1 November as the Feast of All Saints, and it is difficult to discount the view that it was in some way influenced by Celtic custom, which gave such an enormous importance to the Feast of Samhain – the season celebrating the passing over of the dead into the other world.

In the ninth-century Irish martyrology *Felire Oengusso Celi De*, one of the manuscripts gives us this statement: the saints of the teeming world ennoble stormy Samhain. It could be inferred from this that the Feast of All Saints was celebrated in Ireland at an early date and it is believed that the feast spread from here to the continent by way of Northumbria. The Feast of All Saints, again connected with the other world, spread out from the Abbey of Cluny in France in the tenth century.

The period of Samhain, from 1 November to mid–December in the old Gaelic calendar, corresponds with the same period for the preparation of Christmas, i.e. Advent.

Samhain and Bealtaine are the sacred points of the Celtic year, 'the in between periods' in which order and chaos predominate. At Samhain (Halloween) the summer is not quite over and the winter has not yet begun. Samhain is traditionally the beginning of the Celtic year; the dark half of the year comes first, giving place to the bright part – winter giving place to summer and death giving way to life. Samhain is the Celtic New Year's Eve and predictions are made regarding the year to come – whoever finds the ring in the báirín breac, for instance, will be married soon.

Bonfires are lit to assist the sun to keep on shining and to destroy the evils of the preceding six-month period.

Oíche Shamhain is called Oíche na gCleas – the night of the trick – and today we have the custom 'Trick or Treat' in many parts of Ireland. Another known custom, still in evidence today – though in a much more carefree form – is that of groups of people in masks and various other types of disguise going from house to house collecting. Originally they collected money, eggs, bread or whatever the householder had. This was called questing, and it was also a custom of the Wren Boys, around the winter solstice or St Stephen's Day – in the Brídeog Procession on 31 January, and at Scotland's Hogmanay on the same date. It is also well-known in Greek folk-custom.

Traditionally, if the people of the house gave generously, they could expect to prosper throughout the year; if they were mean or stingy they could expect misfortune in the future.

Thus we understand that for the Celts Samhain was very definitely the time when the barrier between this world and the other world crumbled and the time when the dead passed from this world to the one beyond. So it is easy to understand how Christianity replaced this Celtic tradition with the Feasts of All Saints and All Souls.

Celebrating the life of Mary (p.21)

Sketches from the life of Mary

1. THE ANNUNCIATION OF THE BIRTH OF JESUS

Setting: *Mary asleep in bed in a darkened room.*

Voice: Mary, Mary, ...

Mary rubs her eyes with a startled expression on her face, wondering whether she is dreaming or if someone is really calling her.

Voice: Mary, can you hear me?

The room brightens

Mary: *(sits up startled)* Who are you? Who is speaking? *(in a frightened voice)*

Voice: You cannot see me, Mary, but you can feel me, I am a messenger of God.

Mary: A messenger of what?

Voice: God. Don't be alarmed or frightened. God has chosen you to be the mother of the Messiah, the Saviour your people have been waiting for for centuries.

Mary: But I'm engaged to Joseph and what do you think he'd say if I were pregnant before we got married? He'd probably disown me and rightly so. And what about my mother and father? They won't believe that what you say is true.

Voice: Mary, you have been specially chosen. God will not force you to become the mother of the Saviour but you appear to be the most suitable so you are being asked.

Mary: I have prayed to God all my life. Like all my people I have waited for this saviour, and I know that Holy Scripture prophesied that it would be a young maiden who would bear the Saviour of the world, but I never thought for one moment that it could be me. I feel very scared, humbled and honoured.

Voice: Do not be afraid, Mary, God will look after you. It won't be easy telling your parents and Joseph but all will work out in God's time. Go back to sleep now, Mary. All generations will call you blessed.

Mary lies down and goes to sleep.

2. MARY TELLS JOSEPH HER PREDICAMENT

Setting: *Their usual meeting-place beside the well.*

Joseph: You look pale tonight, Mary, is anything the matter?

Mary: *(lowering her head)* No, not really.

She stands up and moves away and says to herself ... How can I tell him? He's such a good man. Will he believe me? What will he do? I love him so. Will he walk off and leave me in disgrace in front of all my family and friends? 'O God of my Father, listen to me and hear my prayer tonight, in my serious situation'. *Walks back and sits beside Joseph who has been watching her closely.*

Joseph:	There is something troubling you, Mary. You are always full of chat and laughter when we meet and tonight there's hardly a word out of you. Tell me, Mary. We'll be married soon so I expect there will be no secrets between us.
Mary:	Oh, Joseph, I'm all mixed up. I have something to tell you but I'm afraid that you won't understand.
Joseph:	Try me.
Mary:	Joseph ... now listen carefully.

Mary tells him about the messenger and the news that she has been given.

Joseph:	*(jumps up)* Do you expect me to believe this? What other man have you been seeing? I thought I was the only one.
Mary:	You are and always have been, and always will be. This is something neither you nor I will understand for a long time, Joseph.
Joseph:	I'm afraid I'm too shocked to take it all in now. My immediate reaction is to leave you and go off, but I'll see. I'm going home now, Mary, and I'll let you know my response tomorrow.

Mary sits alone, sobbing and praying:

O, God, help Joseph tonight to accept what has happened to me as coming from you. He's a good man and I love him and I don't want to lose him. Please, God, do this for me. Amen.

3. THE JOURNEY TO BETHLEHEM WITH JOSEPH

Setting:	*Mary at home knitting, reading, preparing tea – obviously pregnant.*
Joseph:	*(bursts in)* Mary, I have terrible news for you, and I feel dreadful about having to tell you at this time.
Mary:	It's all right, Joseph. I'm not as fragile as all that. What is it? It must be terrible, going by the look on your face.
Joseph:	It is terrible, Mary, for someone as far advanced in pregnancy as you. The Emperor, Caesar Augustus, insists that we all go to our cities to be enrolled. He wants to find out how many citizens there are in his area. This means that you and I have to head off for Bethlehem. It's a very long journey for someone in your condition to have to make and all we have is Neddie, the donkey, and he's not too young either. What will I do, Mary? I can't leave you behind – you have to go with me because you are my wife.
Mary:	Don't worry, Joseph. God will look after us. God is over all, and will see us safely there.

They pack and set off, having locked everything and left a message on the door for Joseph's customers. Moving along quietly ...

Joseph:	Are you comfortable, Mary?
Mary:	Of course I am. Haven't you done everything to make me so?
Joseph:	It's a long journey isn't it? I am sorry about you and our baby. Will you both be safe until the end of our journey?

Mary:	Of course we will. I think I see lights in the distance.

They hear music and singing and come across groups like themselves on their way to sign the register.

They are warmly welcomed and Joseph goes off to find a place for Mary to lie down. Mary joins a group and watches the singing and dancing. (Here there could be a selection of class songs and dances). Sylvia – an older woman – offers Mary something to drink and some motherly advice.

Sylvia:	Keep yourself warm, dear, and don't be eating spicy food. I think you'd need to have a good rest now for the long journey ahead.
Mary:	Yes, I'm quite tired, but Joseph is as good. He worries so much about me. I don't want him fussing too much over me. I think I'll go along to bed now. Thanks for everything – see you in the morning.
Sylvia:	Good night. Sleep well.
Narrator:	They continued their journey in the company of these people and Sylvia kept an eye on Mary, much to Joseph's relief.

4. THE BIRTH OF JESUS

Setting:	*Mary lying down with Joseph attending her*
Joseph:	Mary, I'm ashamed – this is not the way that I expected our child would come into the world.
Mary:	Shush, Joseph. As long as you are there I'll be okay. Oh, Joseph, the pains are getting strong, I think you'd better get the midwife.

Joseph leaves to fetch the midwife.

Mary with some of her friends from the journey, talking quietly. The midwife arrives and sends Joseph out for boiling water. The group surrounds Mary's bed, blocking it out.

Joseph:	*(knocking at the door)* I need boiling water. My wife is expecting our baby.
Doorman:	Who could refuse a request like that? Here's water and plenty more if you need it.
Joseph:	Thank you, and may God bless your generosity always.

Joseph hurries back. As he comes in he hears crying and rushes in to see a beautiful new baby in Mary's arms. He is overcome with joy. The group drop down on their hunkers.

Joseph:	O Mary, our son...
	our son ...
	Praise God ...
	Praise God in the highest.

5. THE CHILD JESUS IS FOUND IN THE TEMPLE

Setting: *Crowds in the market place. Mary and Joseph going around searching for Jesus. Have you seen our boy? He's about twelve, dark hair, tall for his age, mature. We can't seem to find him anywhere. Heads shaking 'no'. Mary and Joseph meet up again with their relatives.*

Mary: I don't know what came over him. He never did anything like this before.

Joseph: He's probably just playing with his friends and lost all track of time.

Mary: Oh, Joseph, what if we never find him again? All those stories you hear about rich merchants stealing children away and the parents never seeing them again. Oh, Joseph ... *(sobbing)*

Joseph: Shush, shush, Mary ... he's very reliable. Whatever he's doing he knows what he's about.

Mary: How could he have us so worried? I can't understand it at all. It must be his age.

    Someone runs up panting ... We've seen him, we've seen him. He's in the Temple talking to all the elders. They have him standing up on a box and all are gazing at him, listening to every word he utters.

Mary: My God? what's he at, we'll never live this down.

Joseph: Trust him, Mary, remember who he is.

    Joseph and Mary rush off to the Temple followed by their friends and relatives. They come to the outer circle of the Temple and can hear him asking questions. In the background is a group of elders, with Jesus in their midst, teaching. Joseph and Mary wait till he sees them and moves towards them.

Jesus: Mother and Father, I've been having a great ...

Mary: *(bursts in)* Son, son, how could you embarrass us like this in front of all our friends and relations? What's come over you? Have you been drinking wine?

Jesus: No, no, no. I'm sorry for upsetting you. I didn't think you'd miss me. I'm doing what my Father in Heaven sent me to do.

    Mary and Joseph look at each other in puzzlement and say together:

Mary & Joseph: But we don't understand.

Jesus: You will, you will. Come along.

    And all three drive off to continue the journey.

6.a. A DAY IN THE LIFE OF MARY AND JESUS (aged 4)

First day at school

Setting:	*Mary, Joseph and Jesus in the kitchen.*
Mary:	Joseph, I cannot believe this day has come.
Joseph:	Yes, our son has grown very quickly and time has flown.
Jesus:	See, I am ready – my new clothes, new bag, new sandals – I hope all my friends will be there. I can't wait to get to school for the first time.
Mary:	Have you got your lunch?
Jesus:	Yes, Mam.
Joseph:	Have a good day, listen and learn well. I'll be looking forward to hearing all your news when you come back. Bye.
Jesus:	*(walks to the door and waves)* See you after school.

Mary and Jesus head off and arrive with the other new children and their mothers gathered excitedly at school gate.

Judith:	Hi, Mary! Is Jesus starting today too? Caspar is my last and I'm going to be very lonely without him.
Mary:	Say 'Hello' to Auntie Judith, Jesus.
Jesus:	Hello, Auntie Judith.
Judith:	Are you looking forward to going to school?
Jesus:	Yes, I am, I can't wait. *(jumps up and down with excitement)*

The bell rings. Chorus of moans from the mothers who tidy the children's hair, straighten their clothes, check to see the children are all right. A few tears are shed.

Teacher:	*(arriving among the group)*

Morning everyone ... beautiful morning for all today. Now, let me see, have I got all the new little children?

Jacob, son of John	present
Jesus, son of Joseph	present
Zacchaeus, son of Barnabas	present
Simon, son of James	present
Paul, son of Zebedee	present
Thomas, son of Bartholomew	present
Judith, daughter of Anne	present
Elizabeth, daughter of Zachary	present

That's it, all present and correct. Now say goodbye to Mams and Dads and we'll get started on our first day at school.

The children turn with a mixture of sadness, excitement, fear and anxiety,
wave goodbye and follow the teacher into school.
The parents move away slowly.

6.b. A DAY IN THE LIFE OF MARY AND JESUS (aged 7)

Setting: *Mary in the kitchen. Jesus coming home from school.*

Jesus: Hi, is my lunch ready? I'm in a hurry. I have a match on down at the lower field.

Mary: What about your homework? Didn't your teacher say you must do your reading every day?

Jesus: Ah, Mam, I'll do it when I get back. I promise.

Mary: Oh, all right, then. Here's your lunch. Off you go, take care and hurry back.

     Mary working around the house. Sounds of a football match can be heard off-stage.

Jesus: *(rushing in)* We won! We won! We beat the best team in the village.

Mary: That's great news, congratulations. Go and change out of those dirty clothes and wash before your evening meal. Your father will soon be home.

Jesus: Right.

7.a. MARY MEETS JESUS ON THE ROAD TO CALVARY

Setting: *Mary and her friend Sarah at the roadside, waiting.*

Sarah: *(Mary's friend)* Do you think this is wise, Mary? Standing here waiting for your son? His appearance may be too much for you.

Mary: How could I not wait for him, my only son, wrongly accused and treated so unfairly by the authorities. I couldn't rest at home knowing that he would be passing by here today on his way to be murdered by the soldiers.

Sarah: I'm just worried for you.

Mary: I know that you are, Sarah. You have been a very good friend to me all along and I know that you only want to take care of me but I'll be all right.

     Noise/clatter/banging

Sarah: They're coming, they're coming. I can't see too well, my eyesight is failing. Oh Mary, will you be all right?

Mary: Shush, Sarah, I'm fine

     Noise comes closer. The soldiers come into view, surrounding Jesus.

Mary: Oh my son, my son. How could they do this to you?

Jesus: You are a brave, strong woman and in time you will understand. Remember the prophecy of Simeon: 'a sword will pierce your soul'. This is it. Take care, Mother, and continue to pray for all God's people. Farewell.

Mary: Farewell, my son. God's holy and blessed will be done.

     Sarah and Mary follow at a distance.

7.b.   MARY STANDS BY THE CROSS OF JESUS

Setting: *A large crucifix or tableau for children.*

Sarah: *(Mary's friend)* I wonder could we do something for him – he looks so tired and beaten.

Mary: I think not. We could do him more harm than good.

Sarah: Look, he's looking at you and ... *(getting excited)* he's trying to say something. Listen!

Jesus: *(laboured speech)* Mother, John is now your son.

John moves towards Mary.

Sarah: He's saying something else.

Jesus: And John, Mary is now your mother.

John and Mary clasp each other.

Mary: He was always such a good, caring son. He is still thinking about me being on my own. *(looking at Jesus)* Thank you, son.

7.c.   MARY WATCHES THE MEN TAKING JESUS' BODY DOWN

Setting: *A group of Jesus' women friends and Mary watching the men taking his body down.*

Mary: Gently, gently. He's suffered enough.

Joseph of Arimathea: We are, Mary. We know how hard it must be for you. *(slowly, slowly bringing the body down)*

Mary bends over and one of the women hands her a damp cloth and she gently rubs his forehead and face, saying:

Mary: You have done your life's work now, Jesus. Rest in peace. I'll miss you but I know you will always be in my heart.

The group of men and women lift the body of Jesus and carry it away to place it in the tomb.

7.d. MARY IS TOLD THE NEWS OF JESUS' RESURRECTION

Setting:	*Sunday morning. Mary is having her breakfast. Loud knocking on her door. Several women burst in, all talking together.*
Women:	Mary, Mary, Jesus is not in the tomb! Jesus is risen ....
Mary:	Would one of you tell me? I cannot make out what you are all saying ...
Mary of Magdala:	*(breathless)* We went to the tomb this morning and found it empty. Peter and John went in and went flying back to tell their friends but I was so upset I sat in the garden crying and someone called me. I thought it was the gardener and I asked him angrily: 'Where have you put my friend, Jesus'? And you won't believe this, he said 'Mary, Mary' ... and I knew immediately it was Jesus. I would recognise his voice anywhere. So he told me to go and tell his friends that he was going back to his Father and that I was to tell you first, Mary.
Mary:	*(smiling)* Thank you, Mary. You are a good friend and I am happy for you that you were one of the first to know that Jesus is no longer dead but lives and will live on in everyone who believes in him and his teaching. The kettle is boiling so let's have breakfast and rejoice together.

(A Resurrection hymn could be sung here.)

7.e. A GLIMPSE AT MARY'S LIFE AFTER JESUS DIED

Setting:	*Mary meets her friends on the way to the well.*
Sarah:	Hi, Mary. It must be lonely at home now without Jesus.
Mary:	Not really. I miss him, yes, but he wasn't at home much this past few years. He was always out and about preaching the 'good news of God's Kingdom', so I didn't see much of him at all.
Sarah:	Well, now, if you need company or someone to have a chat with, you know where I am any time of the day or night. I'll be only too glad to be of help.
Mary:	People have been so good to me. I've hardly had to bake or lift a finger. This is the first time since he died that I have had to go to the well for water – one person or another has got it for me before I have had a chance. The Rabbi calls each day too and apologises for the behaviour of his elders. He is so embarrassed by it all. People are so good.
Sarah:	I'll be off now, Mary. I have a big clear-up to do after the crowd of visitors who were here for the Passover.
Mary:	If you need any help, just call on me. So long, see you at the Temple on Saturday.

Easter Celebration (p.24)

1. Dramatisation of the Seven Last Words

Setting: *Three children standing, arms outstretched (imitation cross). Each arm is held by a child in soldier gear. The crowd is scattered around, kneeling. Silence.*

Mary and a group of women stand in a huddle, each one comforting Mary.

Mary: My son, my son, what have they done this to you for?

Others: Shush, Mary, we might get caught too. You'll be all right, we'll look after you.

Silence

Jesus: *(lifts his head and addresses John)* John, my beloved friend, look after my mother for me. *(Jn 19:29)*

John: I will, I will *(lowers head again).*

John moves towards Mary and places a protective arm around her. Jesus raises his head again.

Jesus: Mary, take care of John as if he were your own son – just as you took care of me *(Jn 19:26)*

Mary: I will, Jesus.

Jesus lowers his head again. Silence.

Individual voices in the crowd:

Voice 1: Pity he can't save himself like he's saved others.

Voice 2: He deserves what he is getting ... disturbing us in the Temple with all his newfangled talk.

Voice 3: Praise God we won't be disturbed any more with his followers singing every night.

Voice 4: It's about time he was caught.

Voice 5: Who did he think he was, anyway? The son of Mary and Joseph giving himself airs and graces. Son of God, how are you.

Crowd: *(slow chant)* Crucify him! crucify him! *Silence. Several times they stop.*

Jesus: Father, forgive them for they know not what they are doing. *(Lk 23:34)*

Silence

The two robbers begin arguing.

Robber 1: Why can't you save us all? You say you have power that we haven't. Save us, for God's sake.

Silence

Robber 2: Keep quiet – you at least are getting what you deserve, you thief. This man is innocent. He has never done anything wrong like you and me stealing people's belongings, breaking into homes, spending other people's money. He's a good man, telling people to love each other and do good. So keep quiet and say your prayers before you die.

Robber 3: *(turning to Jesus)* When you get to your Heavenly Kingdom remember me, won't you, Jesus?

44

Jesus:	(*turning to him and raising his head*) I promise you – you won't be forgotten. (*Lk 23:43*)

Jesus bows his head again. Silence. Three loud bangs on a drum.

Jesus:	(*in a loud voice*) My God, my God, why have you left me to suffer this alone? (*Mt 27:46*)

Jesus lowers his head again. Murmurs in response from the crowd.

Voice 1:	He's angry ...
Voice 2:	He's giving out to God ...
Voice 3:	He's frightened.

Silence

Jesus raises his head.

Jesus:	I am thirsty .... (*Jn 19:28*) *A sponge is put to his lips ... and he makes moves to avoid it or refuse it, saying or mumbling:*
Jesus:	That's not what I need.

and lowering his head he says:

Jesus:	Father, into your hands I place myself and all that I am. (*Lk 23:46*)

He lowers his head and dies.

All sing:	'Jesus, remember me', Taizé, **Workers for the Kingdom**, page 143

2. The journey from the garden (*Matthew 26:36ff*)

Setting:	*A group of three dressed in bright clothes huddle in a corner, snoring and sleeping. Jesus with his arms outstretched, shaking, in a pleading posture ...*
Narrator:	Jesus went with his disciples Peter, James and John to a place called Gethsemane and he said to them, 'Sit here while I go over there and pray'. Grief and anguish came over him and he said to them:
Jesus:	The sorrow in my heart is so great that I am almost crushed – stay here with me and keep me company.
Narrator	He went on a little further, threw himself face downwards on the ground (*Jesus does this*) and prayed:
Jesus:	Father, I am scared. Please, if it is possible, take this cup of suffering from me. Yet not what I want but what you want be done.
Narrator:	Then he returned to the three disciples and found them asleep, and he said to Peter:
Jesus:	How is it that you three were not able to keep watch with me even for an hour? Keep watch and pray that you will not enter into temptation. The spirit is willing but the flesh is weak.
Narrator:	Once more Jesus went away and prayed.

Jesus moves off and kneels down.

Jesus:	My Father, if this cup of suffering cannot be taken away unless I drink it, your will be done.
Narrator:	He returned once more and found the disciples asleep – they could not keep their eyes open. Again he left them and went away praying the same thing. Then he returned to the disciples and said:
Jesus:	Are you still sleeping and resting? Look, the hour has come for the son of man to be handed over to the power of sinful men. Get up, let us go. Look, here is the man who is betraying me. *(Jesus points to Judas.)*
	Group of soldiers, loud noises, bangs, shouts, clangs. Judas, a money bag obviously in his hand, approaches Jesus.
Narrator:	Jesus was still speaking when Judas, one of the twelve disciples, arrived *(pause for Judas to approach Jesus)*. With him was a large crowd armed with swords and clubs and sent by the chief priests and the elders. The traitor, Judas, had given the crowd a signal. *Judas turns back to the crowd.*
Judas:	The man I kiss is the one you want ... arrest him!
Narrator:	Judas went straight to Jesus and said.
Judas:	Peace be with you, Teacher.
Narrator:	He kissed Jesus. And Jesus answered:
Jesus:	Be quick about it, friend.
Narrator:	Then the soldiers came up and arrested Jesus and held him tight *(the soldiers surround Jesus, hold his hands behind his back, and blindfold him)*. One of those who was with Jesus drew his sword and struck at the High Priest's slave's ear, cutting it off *(act this out)*, and Jesus said:
Jesus:	Put your sword back in its place, Peter. All who take the sword will die by the sword. Don't you know that I could call on my Father for help and at once he would send me more than twelve armies of angels? But in that case how could scripture come true which says that all this must happen?
Narrator:	Then Jesus spoke to the crowd:
Jesus:	*(facing crowds)* Did you have to come with swords and clubs to capture me as though I were an outlaw? Every day I sat down and taught in the Temple and you did not arrest me. But all this has happened in order to make what the prophets wrote in the scriptures come true.
Narrator:	Then all his friends left him and ran off *(they dash away in all directions)*. Those who arrested Jesus led him away to be questioned by Caiaphas the High Priest *(Jesus is led away)* and the crowds dispersed.

3. A Conversation between a Soldier and Jesus

Setting: *All have gone to bed after the questioning of Jesus. He is standing tied to the pillar, blindfolded, hands bound. A soldier is on duty sitting near him, speaking quietly.*

Soldier: Hey, why don't you stand up for yourself?

Jesus: There's no need. They will not listen to my words anyway.

Soldier: You are a brave man. Are you really who you say you are – the son of God – or are you fooling us all?

Jesus: Why would I fool anyone? Would anyone want this to happen to them? You know your scriptures. The son of man would be rejected by his own people. I am he.

Soldier: Can you prove this to me?

Jesus: No, but when I die I will rise again. You will only understand this in time. Not now, because your faith is shallow.

Soldier: I'd like to believe it but I'm not ready. My friends would laugh at me and make a fool of me.

Jesus: I know … I understand. But some day you will know and believe that I am truly the son of God.

                There is a noise from the corner.

Soldier: (*pretending to be rough*) Stand up straight there.

                ..fades out …

4. A Conversation between One of the Thieves and Jesus

Setting: *Three people in crucifixion shapes – two robbers and Jesus. Two children are holding up the arms of each of the three, with their backs to the group. The good thief is to the right of Jesus.*

Thief: Hi Jesus, this is me, Tom. Why are they doing this to you? You didn't do anything wrong. All I ever heard was that you went about doing good and preaching about God. Is that true?

Jesus: Yes, but that made the leaders in the Temple mad because the people started listening to me instead of to them. You see, I was telling the people to love their enemies and the Temple leaders were telling them to shun them and I was telling the people that I care for sinners and the Temple leaders had no time for sinners. So, you see, I wasn't too popular with the Temple leaders. They didn't like it that the people were turning away from them and following me.

Thief: Oh boy, I see now. You really wound them up. But it still isn't fair that they should concoct this story to kill you and get rid of you.

Jesus: Don't worry, God can work all things unto good and I know he'll take care of me.

Thief: Will you take care of me when I die?

Jesus: I will indeed. You'll be right there beside me in my Heavenly Kingdom.

Thief: Right.

5. A Conversation between the Women and Jesus

Setting: *A crowd on the road, wailing and noisy. Mary is surrounded by her friends.*

Person in crowd: He's coming – he's coming. Oh look at him, the sweat is pouring out of him and his clothes are stuck to his back ...

Mary's friends put their arms around her.
Jesus appears carrying the cross with soldiers in front and behind.

Soldier: Move on – move on *(crossly).* Out of the way ... make room *(to the crowd).*

Jesus arrives among the women and stops.

Woman I: How are you, Jesus?

Jesus: I'll be all right ... it's not much further now.

Woman II: Can we get you anything? You look really tired and exhausted.

Jesus: Yes, I feel dried up and could do with a drink.

Veronica: Here, Jesus, wipe your face in this ...it'll cool you down a bit. (*A soldier pulls her back roughly.*)

Jesus: Don't be worried, friends ... about me ... be worried for yourselves and your children. The day will come when people will say: well, if things like this are done when I am with you, what will be done when I'm not around?

Jesus is pushed on and the women are left wailing and crying and comforting each other.

6. A Conversation between Mary and Jesus

Setting: *Mary standing with her friends, waiting. The clatter and bang of soldiers approaching with Jesus can be heard.*

Sarah: Be brave, Mary. He needs your strength and support.

Mary: I will, Sarah. You have been very good to me, staying with me all this time.

Sarah: That's what friends are for – to be there when you need them.

Soldier: Make way – make way.

Jesus enters bowed under the weight of the cross. He comes slowly and acknowledges Mary's presence.

Jesus: Mother ... don't wait for all this. Go home. It will be too much for you.

Mary: No, Son, I'll be right here beside you to the end.

Jesus: I'm sorry you have to endure all this.

Mary: Son, I want to be there for you. If you need me, I am here.

Soldier: Move on, move on *(pushing Jesus).*

Mary: Go on, Son, I'll be all right. Our friends have been very good to me.

Jesus: Good *(moves on).*

Mary collapses into the arms of Sarah who supports her.

7. The Final Journey

Dramatise a few stations in a modern version, arriving at the cross.

Setting:	*Narrator; Pilate; Jesus and soldiers; group from the crowd.*
Narrator:	Luke 23:13-26
	Pilate called together the chief priests, the leaders, and the people and said to them:
Pilate:	You brought this man to me and said that he was misleading the people. Now I have examined him here in your presence and I have not found him guilty of any of the crimes you accuse him of. Nor did Herod find him guilty, for he sent him back to us. There is nothing this man has done to deserve death. So I will have him whipped and let him go.
Narrator:	The whole crowd cried out:
Group:	Kill him! Set Barabbas free for us!
Narrator:	Barabbas had been put in prison for a riot that had taken place in the city and for murder. Pilate wanted to set Jesus free, so he appealed to the crowd again but they shouted back:
Group:	Crucify him! Crucify him!
Narrator:	Pilate said to them a third time:
Pilate:	But what crime has he committed? I cannot find anything that he has done that deserves death! I will have him whipped and set him free.
Narrator:	But they kept shouting at the tops of their voices that Jesus should be crucified and finally their shouting succeeded. So Pilate passed the sentence on Jesus that they were asking for. He set free the man they wanted, the one who had been put in prison for riot and murder and he handed Jesus over to them to do as they wished. The soldiers led Jesus away.
	The soldiers lead Jesus away and bring him back with a paper/imitation cross on his shoulder.
Narrator:	Jesus is now condemned to die.
	V. We adore you O Christ and we bless you:
	R⁊. Because by your holy Cross you have redeemed the world.
Reader 1:	Jesus was condemned in spite of being innocent. He had not committed any crime. But the leaders of the Jews wanted to get rid of him because the statements he made clashed with their way of thinking. They objected to the way he spoke and listened to women – showing the same respect to women as he did to men. They resented that he went to eat in the houses of known sinners and they were greatly disturbed that many of their followers were no longer listening to them but following Jesus instead. This frightened them so they planned to remove him from their presence – because he spoke the true gospel of love and service.
	In today's world there are many innocent victims of truth: Salman Rushdie; all those unknown prisoners throughout the world locked up for their beliefs in the dignity and equality of all peoples; those set up and accused of crimes they didn't commit; all the innocent victims of death in the war-torn areas of the world *(list some of these areas).*
	The friends of Jesus abandoned him because they were frightened and afraid. So he had no one to defend him. We pray for all those people today, children, women and men, who are being condemned to death, poverty, homelessness and unemployment, because there is no one to defend them. We pray that we will have the courage to be a voice for the innocent when necessary.

Jesus moves on, pulling the cross. The group hums 'Stay with me', **Workers for the Kingdom,** *page 299*

Narrator: Jesus falls under the weight of the cross.

V. We adore you, O Christ and we bless you:
R⁊. Because by your Holy Cross you have redeemed the world.

Reader 2: Just imagine the heat, the anguish, the pain, the weight of the cross, the shouting of the soldiers and people. This all became too much for Jesus so he fell down flat on his face. There was no one there to help him. All those who would have wanted to were afraid because of their neighbours and the soldiers. So he was left to pick himself up.

We all know how embarrassing it is to fall down in front of our friends and make a fool of ourselves. We don't like it. We wish it would never happen, but it does. We trip on a skipping rope, we fall over school-bags, we cut our knees, we get stuck in the sand, we fall just before the end of the race ... and we don't like it. Jesus didn't like it either and he had no one there to help him get up. We usually have someone – our friends, our parents, our teacher. Today we pray that we will not let the falling down keep us down but that we will be brave like Jesus and pick ourselves up and continue courageously on our way.

The group hums 'Stay with Me'

Narrator: Veronica wipes the face of Jesus.

V. We adore you O Christ and we bless you:
R⁊. Because by your holy Cross you have redeemed the world

Reader 3: By now Jesus would have been perspiring a great deal and he would have felt thirsty. None of the soldiers would have been bothered to attend to him or to worry about him in this way. Some of the crowds watching would have liked to have been able to help but they would have been too scared. Yet out stepped a brave woman named Veronica with a towel in her hand and offered to wipe Jesus' face. Imagine her doing it gently and tenderly while her heart thumped with fear – she could be murdered by one of these soldiers. You can imagine how Jesus felt – relieved at having his face cleaned up, cheered by this woman who had so much courage, and strengthened by her love as he continued his awful journey.

Many times we too are in need of a Veronica in our lives, someone to wipe away our tears, to encourage us when we are disheartened, to cheer us up when we are sad and lonely. Others too need us to be a Veronica for them in their disappointment, pain and sadness. We pray that we will have the courage to be a 'Veronica' to people who need us and that we can have the simplicity to receive the love and care of a 'Veronica' in our lives.

Hymn: *'Whatsoever you do',* **Walk in My Presence,** *page 273*

Narrator: Jesus is stripped of his clothes.

V. We adore you O Christ and we bless you:
R⁊. Because by your holy Cross you have redeemed the world

Reader 4: Remember that there were crowds of people standing around jeering and shouting at Jesus. Remember too that he had carried the cross for a long time in a very warm climate, so his clothes would have been stuck to him. The soldiers would not have been too gentle. They wanted to make a public spectacle of him, so there, in front of all these people, they took off all his clothes and left him naked. He must have been terribly embarrassed and Mary would have been too. We wonder what kind of people could be so cruel that they would do a thing like this. We can all do it. We strip people of their dignity when we gossip about

50

their lives behind their backs, we strip people of their good names when we speak of them as coming 'from that area'. We strip people of their self-worth when we embarrass them because of their accent or their parent's livelihood in front of their friends. We pray that we may remember that each of us is a child of God – unique and different and loved by him and precious in his eyes. We will always try not to strip anyone of their dignity, good name or self-worth.

Narrator: Jesus dies on the Cross.

V. We adore you O Christ and we bless you:
R⁊. Because by your holy Cross you have redeemed the world

Reader 5: The place became very quiet and at the third hour Jesus raised his head and exclaimed, 'it is finished' and lowered his head and died. His work was finished. Mary had said 'yes' to God's word thirty-three years before this. Little did she know what this 'yes' was going to entail of joy, sorrow and pain. Jesus knew how he was going to die. He knew that this was the Father's plan for him. He knew that in dying he was to bring life to all of us. 'In dying he destroyed our death, in rising he restored our life.'

We remember today all our dead friends and those people close to us who are now sharing this wonderful life that Jesus lived and died for, and we pray that each of us will one day enjoy eternal life with all those we love and care for.

6. The Shift from the Adulation of Palm Sunday to the Denunciation of Good Friday

Setting: *Jesus riding along, plenty of singing and dancing, a party atmosphere: psalms, branches, flags, colour, swaying, children wearing white head bands, placards, posters.*

The crowd is singing, eventually singing clearly: 'Alleluia, Praise God in the Holiest', or 'Sing Praise to our Creator', or any 'Holy, Holy, Holy'.

Narrator: Luke 19:28

As Jesus came near Bethphage and Bethany at the Mount of Olives, he sent two disciples ahead with these instructions. 'Go to the village there ahead of you; as you go in, you will find a colt tied up that has never been ridden. Untie it and bring it here. If someone asks you why you are untying it, tell him the Master needs it'. They went on their way and found everything just as Jesus had told them. As they were untying it, the owners said to them: 'Why are you untying it?' 'The master needs it', they answered, and they took the colt to Jesus. Then they threw their cloaks over the animal and helped Jesus get on. As he rode on, people spread their cloaks on the road. When he came near Jerusalem, a large crowd of his disciples began to thank God and praise him in loud voices for all the great things they had seen.

Voice 1: God bless the King who comes in the name of the Lord.

Voice 2: Peace in Heaven and glory to God.

Voice 3: Praise to the Son of God.

Voice 4: Holy, holy, holy Lord, God Almighty.

All finish by singing 'Holy, holy,'

Sudden silence. Head bands changed to black and joyous noises fade out. Jesus standing, arms outstretched.

Voice 1:	Hey, you, why can't you save yourself?
Voice 2:	I thought you said that your Father would send angels to protect you?
Voice 3:	You've got what you deserve.

Chorus, slowly beginning: 'Crucify him ... Crucify him' (in small groups), growing to crescendo, all shouting 'Crucify him, Crucify him ....'

If possible, lighting going from bright to dark.

Hymn:	*'Were you there when they crucified My God?'*

7.   The Story of the Women *(Matthew 28:1–15)*

Setting:	*Two or three women huddled together whispering and looking around constantly, checking on the movements of the guards. Darkness ... (imitation cave)*
Mary Magdalen:	The coast is clear. Look, the guards are asleep.

The women creep towards the cave. Suddenly, lights, banging, the women freeze. They crouch down thinking it is the soldiers about to attack – whispering:

Women:	Save us, O God! Save us, O God!

They hear a quiet gentle voice saying:

Angel:	It's all right, it's not the soldiers. Do not be frightened.

The women slowly lift their heads and look towards an angel sitting in front of the tomb which has light coming out of it. The women cling to each other. The soldiers look as if they've been drugged but can see and hear everything.

Women:	*(in unison, trembling)* Who are you?
Angel:	I have been sent by God to tell you not to keep on looking for Jesus here. Come over and look. The tomb is empty. He is not here. He has risen from the dead. But hurry, go and tell his friends, and remember to tell them that Jesus will meet them in Galilee. Go ... make haste.

The women, afraid yet happy, rush off to tell everyone.

Women:	Jesus is risen. He told us he would. Praise be to the almighty God!

As the women are rushing hither and thither shouting out in joy, they suddenly come to a stop. Jesus is there himself.

Jesus:	Peace to you all. Don't be afraid, go and tell my friends I'll meet them in Galilee.

The women rush off.

The soldiers come to life slowly, and check the tomb disbelievingly.

Soldier 1:	Did you all see and hear what I did?
Other soldiers:	We did.
Soldier 2:	Nobody will believe us.

52

Soldier 3:	What'll we do? Let's ask the elders. *The soldiers move towards the elders and tell their story.*
Elder 1:	Let's say his friends came in the middle of the night and stole his body while you were all asleep.
Elder 2:	Yes, that sounds good. People will believe that.
Elder 1:	And we'll give you a large sum of money to keep quiet, otherwise we will all look terrible fools for having killed this innocent man as we have.
Narrator:	The guards took this money and did what they were told to do. And so that is the report spread round by the Jews to this very day.

8. The Story of Mary of Magdala (John 20:11-18)

Setting:	*Mary of Magdala sitting knitting, wiping a tear from her eye occasionally and talking to herself.*
Mary:	What will I do without him! He was so good to me. I just knew that he loved me. He was a real friend to me. He didn't mind that I wasn't perfect.
	She puts down her knitting and moves cautiously to the opening of the cave. She screams:
Mary:	He's gone! he's gone!
	Turning to the guards she roars at them.
Mary:	Where have you taken him? Tell me and I'll go myself and get him.
	Mary is twisting and turning, tormented, wondering where they would have put him . Suddenly she sees a figure standing there in white. In the half light she thinks it's the gardener.
Mary:	Tell me, did you see where the soldiers took him? I've been here all night and saw nothing and heard nothing.
	Mary running here and there.
Jesus:	Mary ...
Mary:	*Mary swings around and runs towards him, saying gently and joyfully:*
	Rabboni, Teacher! It's you isn't it?
Jesus:	Mary, don't hold me ... I have still to go to the Father ... but go and tell my friends that I am returning to my Father and their Father, to my God and their God. So go and do this for me.
Mary:	Of course, Teacher.
	She dances a joyous dance, picks up her knitting and rushes off, shouting joyfully:
	He's alive! He's alive! I've seen him! He's talked to me!

Separate voices read the following:

Voice 1:   John 20:11-18

Mary stood crying outside the tomb. While she was still crying, she bent over and looked in the tomb and saw two angels there dressed in white, sitting where the body of Jesus had been, one at the head and the other at the feet.
'Woman, why are you crying?' they asked her.
She answered, 'They have taken my Lord away, and I do not know where they have put him!'
Then she turned round and saw Jesus standing there; but she did not know that it was Jesus. 'Woman, why are you crying?' Jesus asked her. 'Who is it that you are looking for?'
She thought he was the gardener, so she said to him, 'If you took him away, sir, tell me where you have put him, and I will go and get him.'
Jesus said to her, 'Mary!'
She turned towards him and said in Hebrew, 'Rabboni!' (This means 'Teacher.')
'Do not hold on to me,' Jesus told her, 'because I have not yet gone back up to the Father. But go to my brothers and tell them that I am returning to him who is my Father and their Father, my God and their God.'
So Mary Magdalene went and told the disciples that she had seen the Lord and related to them what he had told her.

Voice 2:   Matthew 28:9-10

Suddenly Jesus met them and said, 'Peace be with you.' They came up to him, took hold of his feet, and worshipped him. 'Do not be afraid,' Jesus said to them. 'Go and tell my brothers to go to Galilee, and there they will see me.'

Voice 3:   Mark 16:9-11

After Jesus rose from death early on Sunday, he appeared first to Mary Magdalene, from whom he had driven out seven demons. She went and told his companions. They were mourning and crying; and when they heard her say that Jesus was alive and that she had seen him, they did not believe her.

Celebrating our Call to Help People in Need (p.26)

Narrator: We are a group of school friends from Ghana who will speak on different aspects of life in Ghana.

Speaker 1: My name is Uma and I will tell you about our village which is in the north-west of Ghana, not far from Wa. It is divided by a rough, dusty laterite* road. Our houses are square and thatched, with mud walls. They are widely spaced, making the village larger.

In the dry season, the grass withers away, leaving a bare, dusty ground. Our animals grow lanky and bony due to the lack of grass. There is no water supply in the village and in the dry season the women must walk miles to fetch water. Because of the water shortage in the dry season, the people are always very dusty and dirty. It is always a blessing for us in the rainy season. Our animals grow very fat. The village becomes green because of the springing grass. This also makes the village beautiful and the people happy and gay.

In our villages a man's wealth is counted by his cattle. There are many boys to look after the cattle because we have no school. In the dry season the herds must go far to find pasture. The dry season is from October to April. The drought was bad in recent years and families with their surviving cattle came down here from the Sahel region to the north because their own pastures were ruined: All our cattle are for beef. The most common are the big-horned Zebu cattle, which are tougher against disease. The profit from this farming comes from selling cattle in the south, for example Kumasi, where there are many people wanting meat. Cattle cannot be kept in the forest areas to the south because of the tsetse fly. So men take herds of cattle to the south. Many more pass through from Upper Volta to the north, though not so many since the droughts. A man can get double, maybe five times the price for his cattle in Kumasi compared to the local market. But the cattle may become thin or sick, or even die on the long journey and the profit may be lost. Prices in Kumasi go up and down. There are government centres where cattle are checked for disease.

A modern road has been built from Tamale to Kumasi. The bigger farmers can afford to send cattle by truck, but many smaller herds make the journey 'on the hoof' and there are the Fulanis, a tribe of cattle herdsmen, for whom this is a way of life.

And so I hope that you all now know a little more about life in our small village.

Speaker 2: My name is Jude and I will tell how we spend our days in our village. The nearest town is Jumasi, the capital of the Ashanti region in Ghana. It is a small village and the people occupy themselves mainly with farming. There are some mud houses in my village and, of course, some brick houses with beautiful backyard gardens.

We leave our homes for our farms as early as 5.30 a.m. and nothing is more soothing to us children than the cold dew on the grass we walk on. Almost every family has a farm so the village looks deserted between 6.00 a.m. and 2.00 p.m. When we arrive on our farms we make a fire, work on our farms and at about 9.00 a.m. we have our breakfast. We continue working on our farms till about 4.00 p.m. It might surprise you that we have no lunch on the farm. Well, what we do is we drink water from nearby streams and wells when we are thirsty and our breakfast (usually plantain, cocoyam, or yam, or even cassava) is heavy enough to sustain us to the evening.

After a short rest we proceed to our homes at about 4.00 p.m. with food for our evening fufu – evening fufu and not meal because it is what we eat every evening and we enjoy it. We put the cassava and plantain or cocoyam on the fire, wait till it is boiling, then, ten minutes after boiling we remove it from the fire, pound it and then we have our fufu. The soup having been cooked we have our supper. Our fathers eat alone from big earthenware pots. After our supper we group up according to our ages. I mean all of us in the village. You will see the men, big and strong, sitting on their chairs talking, and the children playing games under trees. These gatherings, of course, are more prolonged on moonlit nights.

* Laterite is a type of clay.

The scene on moonlit nights is very beautiful. You find the children singing, excited and of course very happy. The song I liked best had words which, translated into English, went like this:

> The life is hard like the stones that cut
> Our feet on our way to our farms
> The fufu is sweet like the dew that wet
> Our feet on our way to our farms.
> We got the fufu from the farms
> While the stones cut our feet.
> So why then should we cry because of the stones?
> All we wanted is our food.
> Now we have it and thanks be to God.

The older men talk and chat and sometimes we would eavesdrop only to hear a few proverbs, for we like using them ourselves and the old men talk in proverbs.

There are some primary schools in our villages and we loved them all the more because we didn't go to the farm. But then when we were caned in school we wished we were on the farms. I expect you would feel the same about school if you were being caned, wouldn't you?

Speaker 3: My name is Ernest and in our culture the birth of a child is a big occasion for all the community so I will tell you all about it now.

Among the Ga people and almost all tribes in Ghana, the birth of a child is not only a family affair. It is also an important occasion for the whole community. This is because everyone is regarded as an important member of his community. Therefore the Outdooring Ceremony is held to commemorate the inclusion of a child into the community. Exactly a week after its birth, the parents prepare by cleaning their house and its surroundings, finding enough chairs to accommodate the guests, sending invitations, brewing beer from corn to be served on the occasion.

On the day of the ceremony, all the guests are seated in a circle very early in the morning before the sun has risen. The person who will 'outdoor' the child goes to the centre and announces the purpose of the gathering. He pours libation to the gods, thanking them for the child, asks for more blessings for the parents, and also for the success of the ceremony. He calls for the child, and the mother, dressed in white, brings him. The 'outdoorer' holds the child and speaks to him as if he were a grown-up. He recounts the achievements and fame of all the people who have borne the name he is about to receive and advises him to be humble and obedient to his parents if he wants to be successful in life. The child is lowered to the ground and raised three times. On the third time, he is gently dropped on the ground and called by his new name. The mother collects the child and the main part of the ceremony ends.

This is the end of all our stories about life in Ghana.

Suggestion: Have a map and some pictures of Ghana to hand.

56

A DAY IN THE LIFE OF A CHILD FROM KENYA

Interviewer:	Habare? (How are you?)
Jomo:	Masure sana. (Fine, thanks.)
Interviewer:	Can you tell me, Jomo, what you did first thing this morning?
Jomo:	I got up with the sun and went off with my father to check the goats.
Interviewer:	What about your breakfast?
Jomo:	I don't have breakfast. I chew maize and cane sugar as I walk along.
Interviewer:	And then what?
Jomo:	I journey on to school with my bit of wood for the fire and arrive there at around 8.00 a.m., having walked four or five miles.
Interviewer:	Can you describe your classroom?
Jomo:	It's a bit like one of your garages, a square shed with a tiny window on top, very dark inside and we don't have all the lovely pictures that you have on the walls or the books. We are lucky to have one book between several of us. Even pencils are scarce. We have to take turns and wait.
Interviewer:	What do you learn?
Jomo:	Oh we learn many things: English, Maths, Religion, Spelling, Science, Geography – and the girls go to special cookery classes and of course we all love singing. We sing everyday.
Interviewer:	Do you get anything to eat during the day?
Jomo:	Yes, at lunch time we are given soup or maize. Sometimes children bring food from home but not many can do that.
Interviewer:	How do you spend the rest of your day at the school?
Jomo:	School finishes around 3.00. We all play football and games for a while and then hurry off home. Because I am the eldest I have to work on the shamba [small farm] on my return from school – attending to the vegetables such as potatoes and maize. My father tried to grow coffee but it didn't work in our area. The climate didn't suit. I feed the hens for my mother – she brings the eggs to the market each morning. And then I play with my friends until the dark comes. This comes very early in our country. It is suddenly very dark at 6.00, not like your country which goes dark slowly.
Interviewer:	Do you have something to eat then?
Jomo:	Oh yes, I have maize called Ugali, goats's meat and potatoes and a soda. I then wash and scrub myself and go to join my brothers and sisters in our mud hut. By this time I am very tired and I fall asleep and dream about the next day.
Interviewer:	Thank you, Jomo, for all that information. Kwa Heri. (goodbye.) Asante Sana. (thank you.)

MAXIMILIAN KOLBE

1. Childhood

Reader: These two illustrations of the life of Maximilian Kolbe help to give us a picture of what this man was like as a young boy and how his courage and sense of justice continued right through his life to his death. He lived his 'truth in his dying'.

In the first sketch we see how Maximilian, known as Raymond to his family, was a normal young boy – playing, fighting, robbing orchards – that is, until there was an element of unfairness involved.

Scene 1: *Three boys – friends – on their way home from school*

Poldark: Hi, Ray, what are you doing after you've had your lunch?

Raymond: I'll be coming out to play as usual.

Poldark: I have a great plan for today. *(looks around, draws Raymond and other friend close)* You know old Mr Powleski out beyond the village who has a big farm? *(Boys nod)* Did you know that he has big orchards, with big juicy red apples? My cousin Maria who works there told me all about them and also told me that every Monday Mr Powleski goes to town to visit his sick sister in hospital. So what about it – will we have a go at robbing it today?

Raymond and his friend nod enthusiastically.

Raymond: What if we are caught? My parents would punish me for stealing.

Poldark: How could we be caught? The old man isn't there. Anyway, if you haven't the guts, don't bother. Toni and I will go alone.

Raymond: *(reluctantly)* Okay ... I'll be there.

The three separate.

Scene 2: *Later, in the orchard*

Toni: They are really big aren't they? I think I'll be sick if I eat any more.

Poldark: Put some up your jersey

There is a cracking sound.

Raymond: What's that? *(All three stop to listen)*

Poldark: It's nothing, probably a bird swinging on a branch.

Raymond: I'm going home ... it's scary here *(crack again)*. I definitely hear a noise.

Loud Voice: Who's there? Anyone there? I hear you. Come out, whoever you are *(boys freeze)*. *Raymond and Poldark leap up and make a bolt for it but Toni is frozen. He can't move and is caught by Mr Powleski, who marches him home to his parents.*

Narrator: The story doesn't end there. Raymond didn't feel good about his friend being caught, and later that evening he got the courage to tell his parents. He and his father went up to Mr Powleski and he apologised for stealing apples from his orchard.

This incident shows the fair streak in Raymond from a young age. He didn't think it was fair to have his friend take all the blame so he did the brave thing and owned up. Poldark was the coward. Toni and Raymond became great friends.

2. Prisoner 16670

Reader 2:	Years later in a concentration camp called Auschwitz:
	Raymond in the meantime had become a Franciscan priest. He studied very hard to become a doctor of theology and philosophy and loved to tinker with anything scientific or electronic. During the Nazi occupation of Poland he was arrested and put in prison.
Setting:	*Prison site with prisoners working under duress guarded by Nazi soldiers*
Scene 1:	*Ten or twelve prisoners mining, working, shovelling, carrying heavy loads, digging. Soldiers ordering, beating, harassing. Freeze scene except for one prisoner sneaking over the wall and disappearing. Unfreeze. Continue action (you can use sound effects during freeze). Work is called to a halt. All stop.*
Guard 1:	*(rough, loud voice)* All line up.
	The prisoners shuffle into place.
Guard 2:	Prisoner 16660
Prisoner:	Present
Guard 2:	Prisoner 16661
Prisoner:	Present
Guard 2:	Prisoner 16662
Prisoner:	Present
Guard 2:	Prisoner 16663
Prisoner:	Present
Guard 2:	Prisoner 16664
	Silence
Guard 2:	*(in louder voice)* Prisoner 16664
	Still no answer
	The faces of the prisoners remain fixed. In a screech the guard calls out again:
Guard 2:	Prisoner 16664 *(and rapidly calls out the rest of the prisoners' numbers).*
	They are roughly marched back to the prison where they are lined up once again.
Guard 2:	Does anyone know where Prisoner 16664 is?
	Silence
	The guard struts up and down.
Guard 1:	Well, you know what happens when one of your group escapes ... ten of you are taken to Block II, known as Death Block. You will receive nothing to eat or drink and you will die.

The camp-leader, Fritzsch, is large and noted for his extreme cruelty. He walks slowly up and down the line wielding his power. With a careless flick of his fingers he indicates one prisoner then another. An officer standing beside him takes down the number. No sound is heard until a prisoner named Francis Gajownicek cries out that he will never see his wife and children again. A sudden silence occurs. One of the other prisoners steps forward and speaks to the camp-leader.

Fritzsch: What does this Polish swine want?

Fr Maximilian: I am a Polish Catholic priest. I am old. I want to take this man's place because he has a wife and family.

Fritzsch: *(surprised)* Out! *(and he orders Francis back)*

Narrator: This was how Maximilian Kolbe took the place of the condemned man. The ten prisoners were placed in Block II, given no food or drink. Slowly they died one by one. By the third week there were still five alive. Fr Kolbe was one of them. The cell was needed for other prisoners so the authorities ordered the doctor to inject a poisonous acid into the arm of each prisoner. Fr Kolbe offered his arm, praying all the time. He died at 12.50 p.m. on 14 August 1941.

He was cremated on 15 August, the Feast of Our Lady, whom he had loved and prayed to all his life.

By offering to die in place of Francis, Maximilian continued to show the courage he had as a boy when he owned up to robbing the orchard.

Maximilian Kolbe was canonised in 1982.